ON CHRIST AND ANTICHRIST

St. Hippolytus, Bishop of Rome

Translated by: *J.H. MacMahon*
Edited by: *D.P. Curtin*

Dalcassian Publishing Co.

Translated by J.H. MacMahon. From Ante-Nicene Fathers, Vol. 5. Edited by Alexander Roberts, James Donaldson, and A. Cleveland Coxe. (Buffalo, NY: Christian Literature Publishing Co., 1886.)

Library of Congress Cataloging-in-Publication Data

1. As it was your desire, my beloved brother Theophilus, to be thoroughly informed on those topics which I put summarily before you, I have thought it right to set these matters of inquiry clearly forth to your view, drawing largely from the Holy Scriptures themselves as from a holy fountain, in order that you may not only have the pleasure of hearing them on the testimony of men, but may also be able, by surveying them in the light of (divine) authority, to glorify God in all. For this will be as a sure supply furnished you by us for your journey in this present life, so that by ready argument applying things ill understood and apprehended by most, you may sow them in the ground of your heart, as in a rich and clean soil. By these, too, you will be able to silence those who oppose and gainsay the word of salvation. Only see that you do not give these things over to unbelieving and blasphemous tongues, for that is no common danger. But impart them to pious and faithful men, who desire to live holily and righteously with fear. For it is not to no purpose that the blessed apostle exhorts Timothy, and says, "O Timothy, keep that which is committed to your trust, avoiding profane and vain babblings, and oppositions of science falsely so called; which some professing have erred concerning the faith." And again, "You therefore, my son, be strong in the grace that is in Christ Jesus. And the things that you have heard of me in many exhortations, commit to faithful men, who shall be able to teach others also." If, then, the blessed (apostle) delivered these things with a pious caution, which could be easily known by all, as he perceived in the spirit that "all men have not faith," (2 Thessalonians 3:2) how much greater will be our danger, if, rashly and without thought, we commit the revelations of God to profane and unworthy men?

2. For as the blessed prophets were made, so to speak, eyes for us, they foresaw through faith the mysteries of the word, and became ministers of these things also to succeeding generations, not only reporting the past, but also announcing I the present and the future, so that the prophet might not appear to be one only for the time being, but might also predict the future for all generations, and so be reckoned a (true) prophet. For these fathers were furnished with the Spirit, and largely honoured by the Word Himself; and just as it is with instruments of music. so had they the Word always, like the plectrum, in union with them, and when moved by Him the prophets announced what God willed. For they spoke not of their own power (let there be no mistake as to that), neither did they declare what pleased themselves. But First of all they were endowed with wisdom by the Word, and then again were rightly instructed in the future by means of visions. And then, when thus themselves fully convinced, they spoke those things which were revealed by God to them alone, and concealed from all others. For with what reason should the prophet be called a prophet, unless he in spirit foresaw the future?

For if the prophet spoke of any chance event, he would not be a prophet then in speaking of things which were under the eye of all. But one who sets forth in detail things yet to be, was rightly judged a prophet. Wherefore prophets were with good reason called from the very first "seers." (1 Samuel 9:9) And hence we, too, who are rightly instructed in what was declared aforetime by them, speak not of our own capacity. For we do not attempt to made any change one way or another among ourselves in the words that were spoken of old by them, but we make the Scriptures in which these are written public, and read them to those who can believe rightly; for that is a common benefit for both parties: for him who speaks, in holding in memory and setting forth correctly things uttered of old; and for him who hears, in giving attention to the things spoken. Since, then, in this there is a work assigned to both parties together, viz., to him who speaks, that he speak forth faithfully without regard to risk, and to him who hears, that he hear and receive in faith that which is spoken, I beseech you to strive together with me in prayer to God.

3. Do you wish then to know in what manner the Word of God, who was again the Son of God, as He was of old the Word, communicated His revelations to the blessed prophets in former times? Well, as the Word shows His compassion and His denial of all respect of persons by all the saints, He enlightens them and adapts them to that which is advantageous for us, like a skilful physician, understanding the weakness of men. And the ignorant He loves to teach, and the erring He turns again to His own true way. And by those who live by faith He is easily found; and to those of pure eye and holy heart, who desire to knock at the door, He opens immediately. For He casts away none of His servants as unworthy of the divine mysteries. He does not esteem the rich man more highly than the poor, nor does He despise the poor man for his poverty. He does not disdain the barbarian, nor does He set the eunuch aside as no man. He does not hate the female on account of the woman's act of disobedience in the beginning, nor does He reject the male on account of the man's transgression. But He seeks all, and desires to save all, wishing to make all the children of God, and calling all the saints unto one perfect man. For there is also one Son (or Servant) of God, by whom we too, receiving the regeneration through the Holy Spirit, desire to come all unto one perfect and heavenly man. (Ephesians 4:13)

4. For whereas the Word of God was without flesh, He took upon Himself the holy flesh by the holy Virgin, and prepared a robe which He wove for Himself, like a bridegroom, in the sufferings of the cross, in order that by uniting His own power with our moral body, and by mixing the incorruptible with the corruptible, and the strong with the weak, He might save perishing man. The web-beam, therefore, is the pass on of the Lord upon the cross,

and the warp on it is the power of the Holy Spirit, and the woof is the holy flesh wrought (woven) by the Spirit, and the thread is the grace which by the love of Christ binds and unites the two in one, and the combs or (rods) are the Word; and the workers are the patriarchs and prophets who weave the fair, long, perfect tunic for Christ; and the Word passing through these, like the combs or (rods), completes through them that which His Father wills.

5. But as time now presses for the consideration of the question immediately in hand, and as what has been already said in the introduction with regard to the glory of God, may suffice, it is proper that we take the Holy Scriptures themselves in hand, and find out from them what, and of what manner, the coming of Antichrist is; on what occasion and at what time that implores one shall be revealed; and whence and from what I tribe (he shall come); and what his name is, which is indicated by the number in the Scripture; and how he shall work error among the people, gathering them from the ends of the earth; and (how) he shall stir up tribulation and persecution against the saints; and how he shall glorify himself as God; and what his end shall be; and how the sudden appearing of the Lord shall be revealed from heaven; and what the conflagration of the whole world shall be; and what the glorious and heavenly kingdom of the saints is to be, when they reign together with Christ; and what the punishment of the wicked by fire.

6. Now, as our Lord Jesus Christ, who is also God, was prophesied of under the figure of a lion, on account of His royalty and glory, in the same way have the Scriptures also aforetime spoken of Antichrist as a lion, on account of his tyranny and violence. For the deceiver seeks to liken himself in all things to the Son of God. Christ is a lion, so Antichrist is also a lion; Christ is a king, (John 18:37) so Antichrist is also a king. The Saviour was manifested as a lamb; (John 1:29) so he too, in like manner, will appear as a lamb, though within he is a wolf. The Saviour came into the World in the circumcision, and he will come in the same manner. The Lord sent apostles among all the nations, and he in like manner will send false apostles. The Saviour gathered together the sheep that were scattered abroad, and he in like manner will bring together a people that is scattered abroad. The Lord gave a seal to those who believed on Him, and he will give one like manner. The Saviour appeared in the form of man, and he too will come in the form of a man. The Saviour raised up and showed His holy flesh like a temple, John 2:19 and he will raise a temple of stone in Jerusalem. And his seductive arts we shall exhibit in what follows. But for the present let us turn to the question in hand.

7. Now the blessed Jacob speaks to the following effect in his benedictions, testifying prophetically of our Lord and Saviour: "Judah, let your brethren praise you: your hand shall be on the neck of your enemies; your father's children shall bow down before you. Judah is a lion's cub: from the shoot, my son, you are gone up: he stooped down, he couched as a lion, and as a lion's cub; who shall rouse him up? A ruler shall not depart from Judah, nor a leader from his thighs, until he come for whom it is reserved; and he shall be the expectation of the nations. Binding his ass to a vine, and his ass's colt to the vine tendril; he shall wash his garment in wine, and his clothes in the blood of the grapes. His eyes shall be gladsome as with wine, and his teeth shall be whiter than milk."

8. Knowing, then, as I do, how to explain these things in detail, I deem it right at present to quote the words themselves. But since the expressions themselves urge us to speak of them. I shall not omit to do so. For these are truly divine and glorious things, and things well calculated to benefit the soul. The prophet, in using the expression, a lion's cub, means him who sprang from Judah and David according to the flesh, who was not made indeed of the seed of David, but was conceived by the (power of the) Holy Ghost, and came forth from the holy shoot of earth. For Isaiah says, "There shall come forth a rod out of the root of Jesse, and a flower shall grow up out of it." (Isaiah 11:1) That which is called by Isaiah a flower, Jacob calls a shoot. For first he shot forth, and then he flourished in the world. And the expression, "he stooped down, he couched as a lion, and as a lion's cub," refers to the three days' sleep (death, couching) of Christ; as also Isaiah says, "How is faithful Sion become an harlot! It was full of judgment; in which righteousness lodged (couched); but now murderers." (Isaiah 1:21) And David says to the same effect, "I laid me down (couched) and slept; I awoke: for the Lord will sustain me; " in which words he points to the fact of his sleep and rising again. And Jacob says, "Who shall rouse him up? "And that is just what David and Paul both refer to, as when Paul says, "and God the Father, who raised Him from the dead." (Galatians 1:1)

9. And in saying, "A ruler shall not depart from Judah, nor a leader from his thighs, until he come for whom it is reserved; and he shall be the expectation of the nations," he referred the fulfilment (of that prophecy) to Christ. For He is our expectation. For we expect Him, (and) by faith we behold Him as He comes from heaven with power.

10. "Binding his ass to a vine: "that means that He unites His people of the circumcision with His own calling (vocation). For He was the vine. (John 15:1) "And his ass's colt to the vine-tendril: "that denotes the people of the Gentiles, as He calls the circumcision and the uncircumcision unto one faith.

11. "He shall wash his garment in wine," that is, according to that voice of His Father which came down by the Holy Ghost at the Jordan. "And his clothes in the blood of the grape." In the blood of what grape, then, but just His own flesh, which hung upon the tree like a cluster of grapes?— from whose side also flowed two streams, of blood and water, in which the nations are washed and purified, which (nations) He may be supposed to have as a robe about Him.

12. "His eyes gladsome with wine." And what are the eyes of Christ but the blessed prophets, who foresaw in the Spirit, and announced beforehand, the sufferings that were to befall Him, and rejoiced in seeing Him in power with spiritual eyes, being furnished (for their vocation) by the word Himself and His grace?

13. And in saying, "And his teeth (shall be) whiter than milk," he referred to the commandments that proceed from the holy mouth of Christ, and which are pure (purify) as milk.

14. Thus did the Scriptures preach before-time of this lion and lion's cub. And in like manner also we find it written regarding Antichrist. For Moses speaks thus: "Dan is a lion's cub, and he shall leap from Bashan." (Deuteronomy 33:22) But that no one may err by supposing that this is said of the Saviour, let him attend carefully to the matter. "Dan," he says, "is a lion's cub; "and in naming the tribe of Dan, he declared clearly the tribe from which Antichrist is destined to spring. For as Christ springs from the tribe of Judah, so Antichrist is to spring from the tribe of Dan. And that the case stands thus, we see also from the words of Jacob: "Let Dan be a serpent, lying upon the ground, biting the horse's heel." (Genesis 49:17) What, then, is meant by the serpent but Antichrist, that deceiver who is mentioned in Genesis, (Genesis 3:1) who deceived Eve and supplanted Adam (πτεϱνιAdam's heel)? But since it is necessary to prove this assertion by sufficient testimony, we shall not shrink from the task.

15. That it is in reality out of the tribe of Dan, then, that that tyrant and king, that dread judge, that son of the devil, is destined to spring and arise, the prophet testifies when he says, "Dan shall judge his people, as (he is) also one tribe in Israel." (Genesis 49:16) But some one may say that this refers to Samson, who sprang from the tribe of Dan, and judged the people twenty years. Well, the prophecy had its partial fulfilment in Samson, but its complete fulfilment is reserved for Antichrist. For Jeremiah also speaks to this effect: "From Dan we are to hear the sound of the swiftness of his horses: the whole land trembled at the sound of the neighing, of the driving of his horses."

(Jeremiah 8:16) And another prophet says: "He shall gather together all his strength, from the east even to the west. They whom he calls, and they whom he calls not, shall go with him. He shall make the sea white with the sails of his ships, and the plain black with the shields of his armaments. And whosoever shall oppose him in war shall fall by the sword." That these things, then, are said of no one else but that tyrant, and shameless one, and adversary of God, we shall show in what follows.

16. But Isaiah also speaks thus: "And it shall come to pass, that when the Lord has performed His whole work upon Mount Zion and on Jerusalem, He will punish (visit) the stout mind, the king of Assyria, and the greatness (height) of the glory of his eyes. For he said, By my strength will I do it, and by the wisdom of my understanding I will remove the bounds of the peoples, and will rob them of their strength: and I will make the inhabited cities tremble, and will gather the whole world in my hand like a nest, and I will lift it up like eggs that are left. And there is no one that shall escape or gainsay me, and open the mouth and chatter. Shall the axe boast itself without him that hews therewith? Or shall the saw magnify itself without him that shakes (draws) it? As if one should raise a rod or a staff, and the staff should lift itself up: and not thus. But the Lord shall send dishonour unto your honour; and into your glory a burning fire shall burn. And the light of Israel shall be a fire, and shall sanctify him in flame, and shall consume the forest like grass."

17. And again he says in another place: "How bath the exactor ceased, and how has the oppressor ceased! God has broken the yoke of the rulers of sinners, He who smote the people in wrath, and with an incurable stroke: He that strikes the people with an incurable stroke, which He did not spare. He ceased (rested) confidently: the whole earth shouts with rejoicing. The trees of Lebanon rejoiced at you, and the cedar of Lebanon, (saying), Since you are laid down, no feller has come up against us. Hell from beneath is moved at meeting you: all the mighty ones, the rulers of the earth, are gathered together— the lords from their thrones. All the kings of the nations, all they shall answer together, and shall say, And you, too, art taken as we; and you are reckoned among us. Your pomp is brought down to earth, your great rejoicing: they will spread decay under you; and the worm shall be your covering. How are you fallen from heaven, O Lucifer, son of the morning! He is cast down to the ground who sends off to all the nations. And you said in your mind, I will ascend into heaven, I will set my throne above the stars of heaven: I will sit down upon the lofty mountains towards the north: I will ascend above the clouds: I will be like the Most High. Yet now you shall be brought down to hell, and to the foundations of the earth! They that see you shall wonder at you, and shall say, This is the man that excited the earth, that

did shake kings, that made the whole world a wilderness, and destroyed the cities, that released not those in prison. All the kings of the earth did lie in honour, every one in his own house; but you shall be cast out on the mountains like a loathsome carcass, with many who fall, pierced through with the sword, and going down to hell. As a garment stained with blood is not pure, so neither shall you be comely (or clean); because you have destroyed my land, and slain my people. You shall not abide, enduring for ever, a wicked seed. Prepare your children for slaughter, for the sins of your father, that they rise not, neither possess my land." (Isaiah 14:4-21)

18. Ezekiel also speaks of him to the same effect, thus: "Thus says the Lord God, Because your heart is lifted up, and you have said, I am God, I sit in the seat of God, in the midst of the sea; yet are you a man, and not God, (though) you have set your heart as the heart of God. Are you wiser than Daniel? Have the wise not instructed you in their wisdom? With your wisdom or with your understanding have you gotten you power, and gold and silver in your treasures? By your great wisdom and by your traffic have you increased your power? Your heart is lifted up in your power. Therefore thus says the Lord God: Because you have set your heart as the heart of God: behold, therefore I will bring strangers upon you, plagues from the nations: and they shall draw their swords against you, and against the beauty of your wisdom; and they shall level your beauty to destruction; and they shall bring you down; and you shall die by the death of the wounded in the midst of the sea. Will you yet say before them that slay you, I am God? But you are a man, and no God, in the hand of them that wound you. You shall die the deaths of the uncircumcised by the hand of strangers: for I have spoken it, says the Lord." (Ezekiel 28:2-10)

19. These words then being thus presented, let us observe somewhat in detail what Daniel says in his visions. For in distinguishing the kingdoms that are to rise after these things, he showed also the coming of Antichrist in the last times, and the consummation of the whole world. In expounding the vision of Nebuchadnezzar, then, he speaks thus: "You, O king, saw, and behold a great image standing before your face: the head of which was of fine gold, its arms and shoulders of silver, its belly and its thighs of brass, and its legs of iron, (and) its feet part of iron and part of clay. You saw, then, till that a stone was cut out without hands, and smote the image upon the feet that were of iron and clay, and broke them to an end. Then were the clay, the iron, the brass, the silver, (and) the gold broken, and became like the chaff from the summer threshing-floor; and the strength (fullness) of the wind carried them away, and there was no place found for them. And the stone that smote the image became a great mountain, and filled the whole earth." (Daniel 2:31-35)

20. Now if we set Daniel's own visions also side by side with this, we shall have one exposition to give of the two together, and shall (be able to) show how concordant with each other they are, and how true. For he speaks thus: "I Daniel saw, and behold the four winds of the heaven strove upon the great sea. And four great beasts came up from the sea, diverse one from another. The first (was) like a lioness, and had wings as of an eagle. I beheld till the wings thereof were plucked, and it was lifted up from the earth, and made stand upon the feet as a man, and a man's heart was given to it. And behold a second beast like to a bear, and it was made stand on one part, and it had three ribs in the mouth of it. I beheld, and lo a beast like a leopard, and it had upon the back of it four wings of a fowl, and the beast had four heads. After this I saw, and behold a fourth beast, dreadful and terrible, and strong

exceedingly; it had iron teeth and claws of brass, which devoured and broke in pieces, and it stamped the residue with the feet of it; and it was diverse from all the beasts that were before it, and it had ten horns. I considered its horns, and behold there came up among them another little horn, and before it there were three of the first horns plucked up by the roots; and behold in this horn were eyes like the eyes of man, and a mouth speaking great things." (Daniel 7:2-8)

21. "I beheld till the thrones were set, and the Ancient of days did sit: and His garment was white as snow, and the hair of His head like pure wool: His throne was a flame of fire, His wheels were a burning fire. A stream of fire flowed before Him. Thousand thousands ministered unto Him, and ten thousand times ten thousand stood around Him: the judgment was set, and the books were opened. I beheld then, because of the voice of the great words which the horn spoke, till the beast was slain and perished, and his body given to the burning of fire. And the dominion of the other beasts was taken away." (Daniel 7:9-12)

22. "I saw in the night vision, and, behold, one like the Son of man was coming with the clouds of heaven, and came to the Ancient of days, and was brought near before Him. And there was given Him dominion, and honour, and the kingdom; and all peoples, tribes, and tongues shall serve Him: His dominion is an everlasting dominion, which shall not pass away, and His kingdom shall not be destroyed." (Daniel 7:13-14)

23. Now since these things, spoken as they are with a mystical meaning, may seem to some hard to understand, we shall keep back nothing fitted to impart an intelligent apprehension of them to those who are possessed of a sound mind. He said, then, that a "lioness came up from the sea," and by that he meant the kingdom of the Babylonians in the world, which also was the head of gold on the image. In saying that "it had wings as of an eagle," he meant that Nebuchadnezzar the king was lifted up and was exalted against God. Then he says, "the wings thereof were plucked," that is to say, his glory was destroyed; for he was driven out of his kingdom. And the words, "a man's heart was given to it, and it was made stand upon the feet as a man," refer to the fact that he repented and recognised himself to be only a man, and gave the glory to God.

24. Then, after the lioness, he sees a "second beast like a bear," and that denoted the Persians. For after the Babylonians, the Persians held the sovereign power And in saving that there were "three ribs in the mouth of it," he pointed to three nations, viz., the Persians, and the Medes, and the

Babylonians; which were also represented on the image by the silver after the gold. Then (there was) "the third beast, a leopard," which meant the Greeks. For after the Persians, Alexander of Macedon obtained the sovereign power on subverting Darius, as is also shown by the brass on the image. And in saying that it had "four wings of a fowl," he taught us most clearly how the kingdom of Alexander was partitioned. For in speaking of "four heads," he made mention of four kings, viz., those who arose out of that (kingdom). For Alexander, when dying, partitioned out his kingdom into four divisions.

25. Then he says: "A fourth beast, dreadful and terrible; it had iron teeth and claws of brass." And who are these but the Romans? Which (kingdom) is meant by the iron— the kingdom which is now established; for the legs of that (image) were of iron. And after this, what remains, beloved, but the toes of the feet of the image, in which part is iron and part clay, mixed together? And mystically by the toes of the feet he meant the kings who are to arise from among them; as Daniel also says (in the words), "I considered the beast, and lo there were ten horns behind it, among which shall rise another (horn), an offshoot, and shall pluck up by the roots the three (that were) before it." And under this was signified none other than Antichrist, who is also himself to raise the kingdom of the Jews. He says that three horns are plucked up by the root by him, viz., the three kings of Egypt, and Libya, and Ethiopia, whom he cuts off in the array of battle. And he, after gaining terrible power over all, being nevertheless a tyrant, shall stir up tribulation and persecution against men, exalting himself against them. For Daniel says: "I considered the horn, and behold that horn made war with the saints, and prevailed against them, till the beast was slain and perished, and its body was given to the burning of fire."

26. After a little space the stone (Daniel 2:34, 45) will come from heaven which smites the image and breaks it in pieces, and subverts all the kingdoms, and gives the kingdom to the saints of the Most High. This is the stone which becomes a great mountain, and fills the whole earth, of which Daniel says: "I saw in the night visions, and behold one like the Son of man came with the clouds of heaven, and came to the Ancient of days, and was brought near before Him. And there was given Him dominion, and glory, and a kingdom; and all peoples, tribes, and languages shall serve Him: and His dominion is an everlasting dominion, which shall not pass away, and His kingdom shall not be destroyed." (Daniel 7:13-14) He showed all power given by the Father to the Son, (Matthew 28:18) who is ordained Lord of things in heaven, and things on earth, and things under the earth, and Judge of all: (Philippians 2:10) of things in heaven, because He was born, the Word of God, before all (ages); and of things on earth, because He became man in the midst of men, to re-

create our Adam through Himself; and of things under the earth, because He was also reckoned among the dead, preaching the Gospel to the souls of the saints, (1 Peter 3:19) (and) by death overcoming death.

27. As these things, then, are in the future, and as the ten toes of the image are equivalent to (so many) democracies, and the ten horns of the fourth beast are distributed over ten kingdoms, let us look at the subject a little more closely, and consider these matters as in the clear light of a personal survey.

28. The golden head of the image and the lioness denoted the Babylonians; the shoulders and arms of silver, and the bear, represented the Persians and Medes; the belly and thighs of brass, and the leopard, meant the Greeks, who held the sovereignty from Alexander's time; the legs of iron, and the beast dreadful and terrible, expressed the Romans, who hold the sovereignty at present; the toes of the feet which were part clay and part iron, and the ten horns, were emblems of the kingdoms that are yet to rise; the other little horn that grows up among them meant the Antichrist in their midst; the stone that smites the earth and brings judgment upon the world was Christ.

29. These things, beloved, we impart to you with fear, and yet readily, on account of the love of Christ, which surpasses all. For if the blessed prophets who preceded us did not choose to proclaim these things, though they knew them, openly and boldly, lest they should disquiet the souls of men, but recounted them mystically in parables and dark sayings, speaking thus, "Here is the mind which has wisdom," (Revelation 17:9) how much greater risk shall we run in venturing to declare openly things spoken by them in obscure terms! Let us look, therefore, at the things which are to befall this unclean harlot in the last days; and (let us consider) what and what manner of tribulation is destined to visit her in the wrath of God before the judgment as an earnest of her doom.

30. Come, then, O blessed Isaiah; arise, tell us clearly what you prophesied with respect to the mighty Babylon. For you spoke also of Jerusalem, and your word is accomplished. For you spoke boldly and openly: "Your country is desolate, your cities are burned with fire; your land, strangers devour it in your presence, and it is desolate as overthrown by many strangers. The daughter of Sion shall be left as a cottage in a vineyard, and as a lodge in a garden of cucumbers, as a besieged city." (Isaiah 1:7-8) What then? Are not these things come to pass? Are not the things announced by you fulfilled? Is not their country, Judea, desolate? Is not the holy place burned with fire? Are not their walls cast down? Are not their cities destroyed? Their land, do not strangers devour it? Do not the Romans rule the country? And indeed these impious people hated you, and did saw you asunder, and they crucified Christ. You are dead in the world, but you live in Christ.

31. Which of you, then, shall I esteem more than you? Yet Jeremiah, too, is stoned. But if I should esteem Jeremiah most, yet Daniel too has his testimony. Daniel, I commend you above all; yet John too gives no false witness. With how many mouths and tongues would I praise you; or rather the Word who spoke in you! You died with Christ; and you will live with Christ. Hear and rejoice; behold the things announced by you have been fulfilled in their time. For you saw these things yourselves first, and then you proclaimed them to all generations. You ministered the oracles of God to all generations. You prophets were called, that you might be able to save all. For then is one a prophet indeed, when, having announced beforetime things about to be, he can afterwards show that they have actually happened. You were the disciples of a good Master. These words I address to you as if alive, and with propriety. For you hold already the crown of life and immortality which is laid up for you in heaven. (2 Timothy 4:8)

32. Speak with me, O blessed Daniel. Give me full assurance, I beseech you. You prophesy concerning the lioness in Babylon; (Daniel 7:4) for you were a captive there. You have unfolded the future regarding the bear; for you were still in the world, and saw the things come to pass. Then you speak to me of the leopard; and whence can you know this, for you are already gone to your rest? Who instructed you to announce these things, but He who formed you in (from) your mother's womb? (Jeremiah 1:5) That is God, you say. You have spoken indeed, and that not falsely. The leopard has arisen; the he-goat has come; he has smitten the ram; he has broken his horns in pieces; he has stamped upon him with his feet. He has been exalted by his fall; (the) four horns have come up from under that one. (Daniel 8:2-8) Rejoice, blessed Daniel! You have not been in error: all these things have come to pass.

33. After this again you have told me of the beast dreadful and terrible. "It had iron teeth and claws of brass: it devoured and broke in pieces, and stamped the residue with the feet of it." (Daniel 7:6) Already the iron rules; already it subdues and breaks all in pieces; already it brings all the unwilling into subjection; already we see these things ourselves. Now we glorify God, being instructed by you.

34. But as the task before us was to speak of the harlot, be with us, O blessed Isaiah. Let us mark what you say about Babylon. Come down, sit upon the ground, O virgin daughter of Babylon; sit, O daughter of the Chaldeans; you shall no longer be called tender and delicate. Take the millstone, grind meal, draw aside your veil, shave the grey hairs, make bare the legs, pass over the rivers. Your shame shall be uncovered, your reproach shall be seen: I will take justice of you, I will no more give you over to men. As for your Redeemer, (He is) the Lord of hosts, the Holy One of Israel is his name. Sit in compunction, get into darkness, O daughter of the Chaldeans: you shall no longer be called the strength of the kingdom.

35. "I was angry with my people; I have polluted mine inheritance, I have given them into your hand: and you showed them no mercy; but upon the ancient (the elders) you have very heavily laid your yoke. And you said, I shall be a princess for ever: you did not lay these things to your heart, neither remembered your latter end. Therefore hear now this, you that are delicate; that sittest, that art confident, that says in your heart, I am, and there is none else; I shall not sit as a widow, neither shall I know the loss of children. But now these two things shall come upon you in one day, widowhood and the loss of children: they shall come upon you suddenly in your sorcery, in the strength of your enchantments mightily, in the hope of your fornication. For you have said, I am, and there is none else. And your fornication shall be your shame, because you have said in your heart, I am. And destruction shall come upon you, and you shall not know it. (And there shall be) a pit, and you shall full into it; and misery shall fall upon you, and you shall not be able to be made clean; and destruction shall come upon you, and you shall not know it. Stand now with your enchantments, and with the multitude of your sorceries, which you have learned from your youth; if so be you shall be able to be profited. You are wearied in your counsels. Let the astrologers of the heavens stand and save you; let the star-gazers announce to you what shall come upon you. Behold, they shall all be as sticks for the fire; so shall they be burned, and they shall not deliver their soul from the flame. Because you have coals of fire, sit upon them; so shall it be for your help. You are wearied with change from your youth. Man has gone astray (each one) by himself; and there shall be no salvation for you." (Isaiah 47:1-15) These things does Isaiah prophesy for you. Let us see now whether John has spoken to the same effect.

36. For he sees, when in the isle Patmos, a revelation of awful mysteries, which he recounts freely, and makes known to others. Tell me, blessed John, apostle and disciple of the Lord, what did you see and hear concerning Babylon? Arise, and speak; for it sent you also into banishment. And there came one of the seven angels which had the seven vials, and talked with me, saying unto me, Come hither; I will show unto you the judgment of the great whore that sits upon many waters; with whom the kings of the earth have committed fornication, and the inhabitants of the earth have been made drunk with the wine of her fornication. And he carried me away in the spirit into the wilderness: and I saw a woman sit upon a scarlet-coloured beast, full of names of blasphemy, having seven heads and ten horns. And the woman was arrayed in purple and scarlet colour, and decked with gold, and precious stone, and pearls, having a golden cup in her hand, full of abominations and filthiness of the fornication of the earth. Upon her forehead was a name written, Mystery, Babylon the Great, the Mother of Harlots and Abominations of the Earth.

37. And I saw the woman drunken with the blood of the saints, and with the blood of the martyrs of Jesus: and when I saw her, I wondered with great admiration. And the angel said unto me, Wherefore did you marvel? I will tell you the mystery of the woman, and of the beast that carries her, which has the seven heads and the ten horns. The beast that you saw was, and is not; and shall ascend out of the bottomless pit, and go into perdition: and they that dwell on the earth shall wonder (whose name was not written in the book of life from the foundation of the world) when they behold the beast that was, and is not, and yet shall be.

38. And here is the mind that has wisdom. The seven heads are seven mountains, on which the woman sits. And there are seven kings: five are fallen, and one is, and the other is not yet come; and when he comes, he must continue a short space. And the beast that was and is not, (even he is the eighth,) and is of the seven, and goes into perdition. And the ten horns which you saw are ten kings, which have received no kingdom as yet; but receive power as kings one hour with the beast. These have one mind, and shall give their power and strength unto the beast. These shall make war with the Lamb, and the Lamb shall overcome them: for he is Lord of lords, and King of kings; and they that are with Him are called, and chosen, and faithful.

39. And he says to me, The waters which you saw, where the whore sits, are peoples, and multitudes, and nations, and tongues. And the ten horns which you saw, and the beast, these shall hate the whore, and shall make her desolate and naked, and shall eat her flesh, and burn her with fire. For God

has put in their hearts to fulfil His will, and to agree, and give their kingdom unto the beast, until the words of God shall be fulfilled. And the woman which you saw is that great city, which reigns over the kings of the earth.

40. After these things I saw another angel come down from heaven, having great power; and the earth was lightened with his glory. And he cried mightily with a strong voice, saying, Babylon the great is fallen, is fallen, and has become the habitation of devils, and the hold of every foul spirit, and a cage of every unclean and hateful bird. For all nations have drunk of the wine of the wrath of her fornication, and the kings of the earth have committed fornication with her, and the merchants of the earth have grown rich through the abundance of her delicacies. And I heard another voice from heaven, saying, Come out of her, my people, that you be not partakers of her sins, and that you receive not of her plagues: for her sins did cleave even unto heaven, and God has remembered her l iniquities.

41. Reward her even as she rewarded (you), and double unto her double, according to her works: in the cup which she has filled, fill to her double. How much she has glorified herself, and lived deliciously, so much torment and sorrow give her: for she says in her heart, I sit a queen, and am no widow, and shall see no sorrow. Therefore shall her plagues come in one day, death, and mourning, and famine; and she shall be utterly burned with fire: for strong is the Lord God who judges her. And the kings of the earth, who have committed fornication, and lived deliciously with her, shall bewail her, and lament for her, when they shall see the smoke of her burning, standing afar off for the fear of her torment, saying, Alas, alas! That great city Babylon, that mighty city! For in one hour is your judgment come. And the merchants of the earth shall weep and mourn over her; for no man shall buy their merchandise any more. The merchandise of gold, and silver, and precious stones, and of pearls, and fine linen, and purple, and silk, and scarlet, and all thyine wood, and all manner vessels of ivory, and all manner vessels of most precious wood, and of brass, and iron, and marble, and cinnamon, and spices, and odours, and ointments, and frankincense, and wine, and oil, and fine flour, and wheat, and beasts, and sheep, and goats, and horses, and chariots, and slaves (bodies), and souls of men. And the fruits that your soul lusted after are departed from you, and all things which were dainty and goodly have perished from you, and you shall find them no more at all. The merchants of these things, which were made rich by her, shall stand afar off for the fear of her torment, weeping and wailing, and saying, Alas, alas! That great city, that was clothed in fine linen, and purple, and scarlet, and decked with gold, and precious stones, and pearls! For in one hour so great riches has come to nought. And every shipmaster, and all the company in ships, and sailors, and

as many as trade by sea, stood afar off, and cried, when they saw the smoke of her burning, saying, What city is like this great city? And they cast dust on their heads, and cried, weeping and wailing, saying, Alas, alas! That great city, wherein were made rich all that had ships in the sea by reason of her fatness! for in one hour is she made desolate.

42. "Rejoice over her, you heaven, and you angels, and apostles, and prophets; for God has avenged you on her. And a mighty angel took up a stone like a great millstone, and cast it into the sea, saying, Thus with violence shall that great city Babylon be thrown down, and shall be found no more at all. And the voice of harpers and musicians, and of pipers and trumpeters, shall be heard no more at all in you; and no craftsman, of whatsoever craft he be, shall be found any more in you; and the sound of a millstone shall be heard no more at all in you; and the light of a candle shall shine no more at all in you; and the voice of the bridegroom and of the bride shall be heard no more at all in you: for your merchants were the great men of the earth; for by your sorceries were all nations deceived. And in her was found the blood of prophets and of saints, and of all that were slain upon the earth." (Revelation 17, Revelation 18)

43. With respect, then, to the particular judgment in the torments that are to come upon it in the last times by the hand of the tyrants who shall arise then, the clearest statement has been given in these passages. But it becomes us further diligently to examine and set forth the period at which these things shall come to pass, and how the little horn shall spring up in their midst. For when the legs of iron have issued in the feet and toes, according to the similitude of the image and that of the terrible beast, as has been shown in the above, (then shall be the time) when the iron and the clay shall be mingled together. Now Daniel will set forth this subject to us. For he says, "And one week will make a covenant with many, and it shall be that in the midst (half) of the week my sacrifice and oblation shall cease." (Daniel 9:27) By one week, therefore, he meant the last week which is to be at the end of the whole world of which week the two prophets Enoch and Elias will take up the half. For they will preach 1, 260 days clothed in sackcloth, proclaiming repentance to the people and to all the nations.

44. For as two advents of our Lord and Saviour are indicated in the Scriptures, the one being His first advent in the flesh, which took place without honour by reason of His being set at nought, as Isaiah spoke of Him aforetime, saying, "We saw Him, and He had no form nor comeliness, but His form was despised (and) rejected (lit. = deficient) above all men; a man smitten and familiar with bearing infirmity, (for His face was turned away); He was despised, and esteemed not." (Isaiah 53:2-5) But His second advent is

announced as glorious, when He shall come from heaven with the host of angels, and the glory of His Father, as the prophet says, "You shall see the King in glory; " (Isaiah 33:17) and, "I saw one like the Son of man coming with the clouds of heaven; and he came to the Ancient of days, and he was brought to Him. And there were given Him dominion, and honour, and glory, and the kingdom; all tribes and languages shall serve Him: His dominion is an everlasting dominion, which shall not pass away." Thus also two forerunners were indicated. The first was John the son of Zacharias, who appeared in all things a forerunner and herald of our Saviour, preaching of the heavenly light that had appeared in the world. He first fulfilled the course of forerunner, and that from his mother's womb, being conceived by Elisabeth, in order that to those, too, who are children from their mother's womb he might declare the new birth that was to take place for their sakes by the Holy Ghost and the Virgin.

45. He, on hearing the salutation addressed to Elisabeth, leaped with joy in his mother's womb, recognising God the Word conceived in the womb of the Virgin. Thereafter he came forward preaching in the wilderness, proclaiming the baptism of repentance to the people, (and thus) announcing prophetically salvation to the nations living in the wilderness of the world. After this, at the Jordan, seeing the Saviour with his own eye, he points Him out, and says, "Behold the Lamb of God, that takes away the sin of the world!" He also first preached to those in Hades, becoming a forerunner there when he was put to death by Herod, that there too he might intimate that the Saviour would descend to ransom the souls of the saints from the hand of death.

46. But since the Saviour was the beginning of the resurrection of all men, it was meet that the Lord alone should rise from the dead, by whom too the judgment is to enter for the whole world, that they who have wrestled worthily may be also crowned worthily by Him, by the illustrious Arbiter, to wit, who Himself first accomplished the course, and was received into the heavens, and was set down on the right hand of God the Father, and is to be manifested again at the end of the world as Judge. It is a matter of course that His forerunners must appear first, as He says by Malachi and the angel, "I will send to you Elias the Tishbite before the day of the Lord, the great and notable day, comes; and he shall turn the hearts of the fathers to the children, and the disobedient to the wisdom of the just, lest I come and smite the earth utterly." These, then, shall come and proclaim the manifestation of Christ that is to be from heaven; and they shall also perform signs and wonders, in order that men may be put to shame and turned to repentance for their surpassing wickedness and impiety.

47. For John says, "And I will give power unto my two witnesses, and they shall prophesy a thousand two hundred and threescore days, clothed in sackcloth." That is the half of the week whereof Daniel spoke. "These are the two olive trees and the two candlesticks standing before the Lord of the earth. And if any man will hurt them, fire will proceed out of their mouth, and devour their enemies; and if any man will hurt them, he must in this manner be killed. These have power to shut heaven, that it rain not in the days of their prophecy; and have power over waters, to turn them to blood, and to smite the earth with all plagues as often as they will. And when they shall have finished their course and their testimony," what says the prophet? "the beast that ascends out of the bottomless pit shall make war against them, and shall overcome them, and kill them," because they will not give glory to Antichrist. For this is meant by the little horn that grows up. He, being now elated in heart, begins to exalt himself, and to glorify himself as God, persecuting the saints and blaspheming Christ, even as Daniel says, "I considered the horn, and, behold, in the horn were eyes like the eyes of man, and a mouth speaking great things; and he opened his mouth to blaspheme God. And that born made war against the saints, and prevailed against them until the beast was slain, and perished, and his body was given to be burned."

48. But as it is incumbent on us to discuss this matter of the beast more exactly, and in particular the question how the Holy Spirit has also mystically indicated his name by means of a number, we shall proceed to state more clearly what bears upon him. John then speaks thus: "And I beheld another beast coming up out of the earth; and he had two horns, like a lamb, and he spoke as a dragon. And he exercised all the power of the first beast before him; and he made the earth and them which dwell therein to worship the first beast, whose deadly wound was healed. And he did great wonders, so that he makes fire come down from heaven on the earth in the sight of men, and deceives them that dwell on the earth by means of those miracles which he had power to do in the sight of the beast, saying to them that dwell on the earth, that they should make an image to the beast which had the wound by a sword and did live. And he had power to give life unto the image of the beast, that the image of the beast should both speak, and cause that as many as would not worship the image of the beast should be killed. And he caused all, both small and great, rich and poor, free and bond, to receive a mark in their right hand or in their forehead; and that no man might buy or sell, save he that had the mark, the name of the beast, or the number of his name. Here is wisdom. Let him that has understanding count the number of the beast; for if is the number of a man, and his number is six hundred threescore and six."

49. By the beast, then, coming up out of the earth, he means the kingdom of Antichrist; and by the two horns he means him and the false prophet after him. And in speaking of "the horns being like a lamb," he means that he will make himself like the Son of God, and set himself forward as king. And the terms, "he spoke like a dragon," mean that he is a deceiver, and not truthful. And the words, "he exercised all the power of the first beast before him, and caused the earth and them which dwell therein to worship the first beast, whose deadly wound was healed," signify that, after the manner of the law of Augustus, by whom the empire of Rome was established, he too will rule and govern, sanctioning everything by it, and taking greater glory to himself. For this is the fourth beast, whose head was wounded and healed again, in its being broken up or even dishonoured, and partitioned into four crowns; and he then (Antichrist) shall with knavish skill heal it, as it were, and restore it. For this is what is meant by the prophet when he says, "He will give life unto the image, and the image of the beast will speak." For he will act with vigour again, and prove strong by reason of the laws established by him; and he will cause all those who will not worship the image of the beast to be put to death. Here the faith and the patience of the saints will appear, for he says: "And he will cause all, both small and great, rich and poor, free and bond, to receive a mark in their right hand or in their forehead; that no man might buy or sell, save he that had the mark, the name of the beast, or the number of his name." For, being full of guile, and exalting himself against the servants of God, with the wish to afflict them and persecute them out of the world, because they give not glory to him, he will order incense-pans to be set up by all everywhere, that no man among the saints may be able to buy or sell without first sacrificing; for this is what is meant by the mark received upon the right hand. And the word— "in their forehead"— indicates that all are crowned, and put on a crown of fire, and not of life, but of death. For in this wise, too, did Antiochus Epiphanes the king of Syria, the descendant of Alexander of Macedon, devise measures against the Jews. He, too, in the exaltation of his heart, issued a decree in those times, that "all should set up shrines before their doors, and sacrifice, and that they should march in procession to the honour of Dionysus, waving chaplets of ivy; "and that those who refused obedience should be put to death by strangulation and torture. But he also met his due recompense at the hand of the Lord, the righteous Judge and all-searching God; for he died eaten up of worms. And if one desires to inquire into that more accurately, he will find it recorded in the books of the Maccabees.

50. But now we shall speak of what is before us. For such measures will he, too, devise, seeking to afflict the saints in every way. For the prophet and apostle says: "Here is wisdom, Let him that has understanding count the number of the beast; for it is the number of a man, and his number is six

hundred threescore and six." With respect to his name, it is not in our power to explain it exactly, as the blessed John understood it and was instructed about it, but only to give a conjectural account of it; for when he appears, the blessed one will show us what we seek to know. Yet as far as our doubtful apprehension of the matter goes, we may speak. Many names indeed we find, the letters of which are the equivalent of this number: such as, for instance, the word Titan, an ancient and notable name; or Evanthas, for it too makes up the same number; and many others which might be found. But, as we have already said, the wound of the first beast was healed, and he (the second beast) was to make the image speak, that is to say, he should be powerful; and it is manifest to all that those who at present still hold the power are Latins. If, then, we take the name as the name of a single man, it becomes Latinus. Wherefore we ought neither to give it out as if this were certainly his name, nor again ignore the fact that he may not be otherwise designated. But having the mystery of God in our heart, we ought in fear to keep faithfully what has been told us by the blessed prophets, in order that when those things come to pass, we may be prepared for them, and not deceived. For when the times advance, he too, of whom these thing are said, will be manifested.

51. But not to confine ourselves to these words and arguments alone, for the purpose of convincing those who love to study the oracles of God, we shall demonstrate the matter by many other proofs. For Daniel says, "And these shall escape out of his hand, even Edom, and Moab, and the chief of the children of Ammon." Ammon and Moab are the children born to Lot by his daughters, and their race survives even now. And Isaiah says: "And they shall fly in the boats of strangers, plundering the sea together, and (they shall spoil) them of the east: and they shall lay hands upon Moab first; and the children of Ammon shall first obey them."

52. In those times, then, he shall arise and meet them. And when he has overmastered three horns out of the ten in the array of war, and has rooted these out, viz., Egypt, and Libya, and Ethiopia, and has got their spoils and trappings, and has brought the remaining horns which suffer into subjection, he will begin to be lifted up in heart, and to exalt himself against God as master of the whole world. And his first expedition will be against Tyre and Berytus, and the circumjacent territory. For by storming these cities first he will strike terror into the others, as Isaiah says, "Be ashamed, O Sidon; the sea has spoken, even the strength of the sea has spoken, saying, I travailed not, nor brought forth children; neither did I nurse up young men, nor bring up virgins. But when the report comes to Egypt, pain shall seize them for Tyre."

53. These things, then, shall be in the future, beloved; and when the three horns are cut off, he will begin to show himself as God, as Ezekiel has said aforetime: "Because your heart has been lifted up, and you have said, I am God." And to the like effect Isaiah says: "For you have said in your heart, I will ascend into heaven, I will exalt my throne above the stars of heaven: I will be like the Most High. Yet now you shall be brought down to hell (Hades), to the foundations of the earth." In like manner also Ezekiel: "Will you yet say to those who slay you, I am God? But you (shall be) a man, and no God."

54. As his tribe, then, and his manifestation, and his destruction, have been set forth in these words, and as his name has also been indicated mystically, let us look also at his action. For he will call together all the people to himself, out of every country of the dispersion, making them his own, as though they were his own children, and promising to restore their country, and establish again their kingdom and nation, in order that he may be worshipped by them as God, as the prophet says: "He will collect his whole kingdom, from the rising of the sun even to its setting: they whom he summons and they whom he does not summon shall march with him." And Jeremiah speaks of him thus in a parable: "The partridge cried, (and) gathered what he did not hatch, making himself riches without judgment: in the midst of his days they shall leave him, and at his end he shall be a fool."

55. It will not be detrimental, therefore, to the course of our present argument, if we explain the art of that creature, and show that the prophet has not spoken without a purpose in using the parable (or similitude) of the creature. For as the partridge is a vainglorious creature, when it sees near at hand the nest of another partridge with young in it, and with the parent-bird away on the wing in quest of food, it imitates the cry of the other bird, and calls the young to itself; and they, taking it to be their own parent, run to it. And it delights itself proudly in the alien pullets as in its own. But when the real parent-bird returns, and calls them with its own familiar cry, the young recognise it, and forsake the deceiver, and betake themselves to the real parent. This thing, then, the prophet has adopted as a simile, applying it in a similar manner to Antichrist. For he will allure mankind to himself, wishing to gain possession of those who are not his own, and promising deliverance to all, while he is unable to save himself.

56. He then, having gathered to himself the unbelieving everywhere throughout the world, comes at their call to persecute the saints, their enemies and antagonists, as the apostle and evangelist says: "There was in a city a judge, which feared not God, neither regarded man: and there was a widow in that city, who came unto him, saying, Avenge me of mine adversary.

And he would not for a while: but afterward he said within himself, Though I fear not God, nor regard man; yet because this widow troubles me, I will avenge her."

57. By the unrighteous judge, who fears not God, neither regards man, he means without doubt Antichrist, as he is a son of the devil and a vessel of Satan. For when he has the power, he will begin to exalt himself against God, neither in truth fearing God, nor regarding the Son of God, who is the Judge of all. And in saying that there was a widow in the city, he refers to Jerusalem itself, which is a widow indeed, forsaken of her perfect, heavenly spouse, God. She calls Him her adversary, and not her Saviour; for she does not understand that which was said by the prophet Jeremiah: "Because they obeyed not the truth, a spirit of error shall speak then to this people and to Jerusalem." And Isaiah also to the like effect: "Forasmuch as the people refuses to drink the water of Siloam that goes softly, but chooses to have Rasin and Romeliah's son as king over you: therefore, lo, the Lord brings up upon you the water of the river, strong and full, even the king of Assyria." By the king he means metaphorically Antichrist, as also another prophet says: "And this man shall be the peace from me, when the Assyrian shall come up into your land, and when he shall tread in your mountains."

58. And in like manner Moses, knowing beforehand that the people would reject and disown the true Saviour of the world, and take part with error, and choose an earthly king, and set the heavenly King at nought, says: "Is not this laid up in store with me, and sealed up among my treasures? In the day of vengeance I will recompense (them), and in the time when their foot shall slide." They did slide, therefore, in all things, as they were found to be in harmony with the truth in nothing: neither as concerns the law, because they became transgressors; nor as concerns the prophets, because they cut off even the prophets themselves; nor as concerns the voice of the Gospels, because they crucified the Saviour Himself; nor in believing the apostles, because they persecuted them. At all times they showed themselves enemies and betrayers of the truth, and were found to be haters of God, and not lovers of Him; and such they shall be then when they find opportunity: for, rousing themselves against the servants of God, they will seek to obtain vengeance by the hand of a mortal man. And he, being puffed up with pride by their subserviency, will begin to dispatch missives against the saints, commanding to cut them all off everywhere, on the ground of their refusal to reverence and worship him as God, according to the word of Esaias: "Woe to the wings of the vessels of the land, beyond the rivers of Ethiopia: (woe to him) who sends sureties by the sea, and letters of papyrus (upon the water; for nimble messengers will go) to a nation anxious and expectant, and a people strange and bitter against them; a nation hopeless and trodden down."

59. But we who hope for the Son of God are persecuted and trodden down by those unbelievers. For the wings of the vessels are the churches; and the sea is the world, in which the Church is set, like a ship tossed in the deep, but not destroyed; for she has with her the skilled Pilot, Christ. And she bears in her midst also the trophy (which is erected) over death; for she carries with her the cross of the Lord. For her prow is the east, and her stern is the west, and her hold is the south, and her tillers are the two Testaments; and the ropes that stretch around her are the love of Christ, which binds the Church; and the net which she bears with her is the layer of the regeneration which renews the believing, whence too are these glories. As the wind the Spirit from heaven is present, by whom those who believe are sealed: she has also anchors of iron accompanying her, viz., the holy commandments of Christ Himself, which are strong as iron. She has also mariners on the right and on the left, assessors like the holy angels, by whom the Church is always governed and defended. The ladder in her leading up to the sailyard is an emblem of the passion of Christ, which brings the faithful to the ascent of heaven. And the top-sails aloft upon the yard are the company of prophets, martyrs, and apostles, who have entered into their rest in the kingdom of Christ.

60. Now, concerning the tribulation of the persecution which is to fall upon the Church from the adversary, John also speaks thus: "And I saw a great and wondrous sign in heaven; a woman clothed with the sun, and the moon under her feet, and upon her head a crown of twelve stars. And she, being with child, cries, travailing in birth, and pained to be delivered. And the dragon stood before the woman which was ready to be delivered, for to devour her child as soon as it was born. And she brought forth a man-child, who is to rule all the nations: and the child was caught up unto God and to His throne. And the woman fled into the wilderness, where she has the place prepared of God, that they should feed her there a thousand two hundred and threescore days. And then when the dragon saw it, he persecuted the woman which brought forth the man- child. And to the woman were given two wings of the great eagle, that she might fly into the wilderness, where she is nourished for a time, and times, and half a time, from the face of the serpent. And the serpent cast (out of his mouth water as a flood after the woman, that he might cause her to be carried away of the flood. And the earth helped the woman, and opened her mouth, and swallowed up the flood which the dragon cast) out of his mouth. And the dragon was angry with the woman, and went to make war with the saints of her seed, which keep the commandments of God, and have the testimony of Jesus."

61. By the woman then clothed with the sun, he meant most manifestly the Church, endued with the Father's word, whose brightness is above the sun. And by the "moon under her feet" he referred to her being adorned, like the moon, with heavenly glory. And the words, "upon her head a crown of twelve stars," refer to the twelve apostles by whom the Church was founded. And those, "she, being with child, cries, travailing in birth, and pained to be delivered," mean that the Church will not cease to bear from her heart the Word that is persecuted by the unbelieving in the world. "And she brought forth," he says, "a man-child, who is to rule all the nations; "by which is meant that the Church, always bringing forth Christ, the perfect man-child of God, who is declared to be God and man, becomes the instructor of all the nations. And the words, "her child was caught up unto God and to His throne," signify that he who is always born of her is a heavenly king, and not an earthly; even as David also declared of old when he said, "The Lord said unto my Lord, Sit at my right hand, until I make Your enemies Your footstool." "And the dragon," he says, "saw and persecuted the woman which brought forth the man- child. And to the woman were given two wings of the great eagle, that she might fly into the wilderness, where she is nourished for a time, and times, and half a time, from the face of the serpent." That refers to the one thousand two hundred and threescore days (the half of the week) during which the tyrant is to reign and persecute the Church, which flees from city to city, and seeks conceal-meat in the wilderness among the mountains, possessed of no other defence than the two wings of the great eagle, that is to say, the faith of Jesus Christ, who, in stretching forth His holy hands on the holy tree, unfolded two wings, the right and the left, and called to Him all who believed upon Him, and covered them as a hen her chickens. For by the mouth of Malachi also He speaks thus: "And unto you that fear my name shall the Sun of righteousness arise with healing in His wings."

62. The Lord also says, "When you shall see the abomination of desolation stand in the holy place (whoso reads, let him understand), then let them which be in Judea flee into the mountains, and let him which is on the housetop not come down to take his clothes; neither let him which is in the field return back to take anything out of his house. And woe unto them that are with child, and to them that give suck, in those days! For then shall be great tribulation, such as was not since the beginning of the world. And except those days should be shortened, there should no flesh be saved." And Daniel says, "And they shall place the abomination of desolation a thousand two hundred and ninety days. Blessed is he that waits, and comes to the thousand two hundred and ninety-five days."

63. And the blessed Apostle Paul, writing to the Thessalonians, says: "Now we beseech you, brethren, concerning the coming of our Lord Jesus Christ, and our gathering together at it, that you be not soon shaken in mind, or be troubled, neither by spirit, nor by word, nor by letters as from us, as that the day of the Lord is at hand. Let no man deceive you by any means; for (that day shall not come) except there come the falling away first, and that man of sin be revealed, the son of perdition, who opposes and exalts himself above all that is called God, or that is worshipped: so that he sits in the temple of God, showing himself that he is God. Do you not remember that when I was yet with you, I told you these things? And now you know what withholds, that he might be revealed in his time. For the mystery of iniquity does already work; only he who now lets (will let), until he be taken out of the way. And then shall that wicked be revealed, whom the Lord Jesus shall consume with the Spirit of His mouth, and shall destroy with the brightness of His coming: (even him) whose coming is after the working of Satan, with all power, and signs, and lying wonders, and with all deceivableness of unrighteousness in them that perish; because they received not the love of the truth. And for this cause God shall send them strong delusion, that they should believe a lie: that they all might be damned who believed not the truth, but had pleasure in unrighteousness." And Esaias says, "Let the wicked be cut off, that he behold not the glory of the Lord."

64. These things, then, being to come to pass, beloved, and the one week being divided into two parts, and the abomination of desolation being manifested then, and the two prophets and forerunners of the Lord having finished their course, and the whole world finally approaching the consummation, what remains but the coming of our Lord and Saviour Jesus Christ from heaven, for whom we have looked in hope? Who shall bring the conflagration and just judgment upon all who have refused to believe in Him. For the Lord says, "And when these things begin to come to pass, then look up, and lift up your heads; for your redemption draws near." "And there shall not a hair of your head perish." "For as the lightning comes out of the east, and shines even unto the west, so shall also the coming of the Son of man be. For wheresoever the carcass is, there will the eagles be gathered together." Now the fall took place in paradise; for Adam fell there. And He says again, "Then shall the Son of man send His angels, and they shall gather together

His elect from the four winds of heaven." And David also, in announcing prophetically the judgment and coming of the Lord, says, "His going forth is from the end of the heaven, and His circuit unto the end of the heaven: and there is no one hid from the heat thereof." By the heat he means the conflagration. And Esaias speaks thus: "Come, my people, enter into your chamber, (and) shut your door: hide yourself as it were for a little moment, until the indignation of the Lord be overpast." And Paul in like manner: "For the wrath of God is revealed from heaven against all ungodliness and unrighteousness of men, who hold the truth of God in unrighteousness."

65. Moreover, concerning the resurrection and the kingdom of the saints, Daniel says, "And many of them that sleep in the dust of the earth shall arise, some to everlasting life, (and some to shame and everlasting contempt)." Esaias says, "The dead men shall arise, and they that are in their tombs shall awake; for the dew from you is healing to them." The Lord says, "Many in that day shall hear the voice of the Son of God, and they that hear shall live." And the prophet says, "Awake, you that sleepest, and arise from the dead, and Christ shall give you light." And John says, "Blessed and holy is he that has part in the first resurrection: on such the second death has no power." For the second death is the lake of fire that burns. And again the Lord says, "Then shall the righteous shine forth as the sun shines in his glory." And to the saints He will say, "Come, you blessed of my Father, inherit the kingdom prepared for you from the foundation of the world." But what says He to the wicked? "Depart from me, you cursed, into everlasting fire, prepared for the devil and his angels, which my Father has prepared." And John says, "Without are dogs, and sorcerers, and whoremongers, and murderers, and idolaters, and whosoever makes and loves a lie; for your part is in the hell of fire." And in like manner also Esaias: "And they shall go forth and look upon the carcasses of the men that have transgressed against me. And their worm shall not die, neither shall their fire be quenched; and they shall be for a spectacle to all flesh."

66. Concerning the resurrection of the righteous, Paul also speaks thus in writing to the Thessalonians: "We would not have you to be ignorant concerning them which are asleep, that you sorrow not even as others which have no hope. For if we believe that Jesus died and rose again, even so them also which sleep in Jesus will God bring with Him. For this we say unto you by the word of the Lord, that we which are alive (and) remain unto the coming of the Lord, shall not prevent them which are asleep. For the Lord Himself shall descend from heaven with a shout, with the voice and trump of God, and the dead in Christ shall rise first. Then we which are alive (and) remain shall be caught up together with them in the clouds to meet the Lord in the air; and so shall we ever be with the Lord."

67. These things, then, I have set shortly before you, O Theophilus, drawing them from Scripture itself, in order that, maintaining in faith what is written, and anticipating the things that are to be, you may keep yourself void of offense both toward God and toward men, "looking for that blessed hope and appearing of our God and Saviour," when, having raised the saints among us, He will rejoice with them, glorifying the Father. To Him be the glory unto the endless ages of the ages. Amen.

www.ingramcontent.com/pod-product-compliance
Lightning Source LLC
Chambersburg PA
CBHW070956120626
46546CB00004B/1643